PERFECTIONISM

31-Day Devotionals for Life

A Series

Deepak Reju
Series Editor

Addictive Habits, by David R. Dunham
After an Affair, by Michael Scott Gembola
After Cancer, by Marissa Henley
Anger, by Robert D. Jones
Anxiety, by Paul Tautges
Assurance, by William P. Smith
Chronic Illness, by Esther Smith
Contentment, by Megan Hill
Depression, by Edward T. Welch
Doubt, by Elyse Fitzpatrick
Engagement, by Mike McKinley
Fearing Others, by Zach Schlegel
Forgiveness, by Hayley Satrom
Grief, by Bob Kellemen
Hope, by John Crotts
Marriage Conflict, by Steve Hoppe
Money, by Jim Newheiser
A Painful Past, by Lauren Whitman
Parenting & Disabilities, by Stephanie O. Hubach
Patience, by Megan Hill
Perfectionism, by Lou Priolo
Pornography, by Deepak Reju
Rest, Heather Nelson
Shame, by Esther Liu
Singleness, by Jenilyn Swett
Toxic Relationships, by Ellen Mary Dykas
Wayward Children, by Stuart W. Scott

I know what it is to be bound by "all-or-nothing" thinking. The havoc it wreaks in our lives is relationally and spiritually destructive. In this book, Lou helps us to pivot away from the bondage of perfectionism and toward the freedom of Spirit-empowered progress. Do you struggle with self-condemnation, self-loathing, or even self-hatred at times? If so, this guide will serve you well. I've been waiting for a resource like this and will refer to it regularly in my ministry to women.
—**Christine Chappell**, Author, *Midnight Mercies*; *Hope + Help Podcast* Host, Institute for Biblical Counseling & Discipleship

It can be frustrating to chase perfection and constantly fail. Lou Priolo shows that the very pursuit of perfection can be the problem. Priolo carefully and comprehensively describes the problem of perfectionism—down to the heart level. Then he offers clear, practical ways to change. There are gospel reasons to hope that you can become a faithful man or woman and truly please the Lord. This resource is a wise and helpful guide.
—**John Crotts**, Pastor; Author, *Hope* (31-Day Devotionals for Life)

"Not that I have already obtained this or am already perfect, but I press on" (Phil. 3:12 ESV). That was the apostle Paul's confession. He further declared his own imperfection as emphatically as possible in Romans 7, calling himself "wretched." Honest believers understand that only Christ is perfect. Indeed, one of the indelible marks of all true Christians is that we freely confess our own imperfections and press on, cultivating a vibrant, active conscience that is shaped and informed by Scripture. Lou Priolo's monthlong daily devotional on perfectionism is a wonderfully practical help for any Christian who is grappling with these issues.
—**John MacArthur**, Pastor-Teacher, Grace Community Church, Sun Valley, California

Lou reminds us that while it is good to strive to be faithful, our perfection is found solely in Christ. A unique feature of this devotional is the practical exercises and diagrams. I look forward to sharing this with my counselees (many of whom struggle with this issue) and to using it in our family devotions.
—**Jim Newheiser**, Executive Director, The Institute for Biblical Counseling and Discipleship

Lou Priolo taught me *how* to be a biblical counselor and showed me *what* it means to live a life that glorifies God. I was privileged to work with Lou for eight years at the Atlanta Biblical Counseling Center. During that time, Lou was instrumental in helping me compose *The Excellent Wife*. When I found out that Lou was critically ill, I also found that he was finishing writing this book on perfectionism. It is especially sweet that the Lord enabled Lou to finish this project mere days before he died. Lou knew that only God can make us perfect and only when He takes us to be with Him in glory. Lou is experiencing truly sinless perfection right now face-to-face with his beloved Savior. This book on perfection is wonderful, and I am so thankful to the Lord that He allowed Lou finish this project. This is a book that I *highly* recommend, and I will recommend it often.
—**Martha Peace**, Author, *The Excellent Wife*; ACBC Certified Biblical Counselor

As one who has struggled with perfectionism and its under-the-surface fears for much of my life, I am indebted to Lou Priolo. In this heart-searching devotional, he helps us to look through biblical lenses and, ultimately, at the sufficiency of Christ and His work on our behalf. His biblical counsel will help many strugglers learn to rest in Jesus and walk in wisdom and grace.
—**Paul Tautges**, Pastor; Counselor; Author, *Remade*

PERFECTIONISM

PURSUING EXCELLENCE WITH WISDOM

LOU PRIOLO

P U B L I S H I N G
P.O. BOX 817 • PHILLIPSBURG • NEW JERSEY 08865-0817

Scripture quotations from the ESV use its alternate, footnoted translation of *adelphoi* ("brothers and sisters").

Italics within Scripture quotations indicate emphasis added.

Printed in the United States of America

Library of Congress Cataloging-in-Publication Data

Names: Priolo, Lou, author.
Title: Perfectionism : pursuing excellence with wisdom / Lou Priolo.
Description: Phillipsburg, New Jersey : P&R Publishing Company, [2024] | Series: 31-day devotionals for life | Includes bibliographical references. | Summary: "A desire to excel may be rooted in love for God-or in something more problematic. Use this devotional to identify your motivations and embrace God's freeing wisdom for your life"-- Provided by publisher.
Identifiers: LCCN 2024010235 | ISBN 9781629957173 (paperback) | ISBN 9781629957203 (epub)
Subjects: LCSH: Perfectionism (Personality trait)--Religious aspects--Christianity. | Devotional calendars.
Classification: LCC BV4597.58.P47 P47 2024 | DDC 242/.2--dc23/eng/20240513
LC record available at https://lccn.loc.gov/2024010235

Contents

How to Nourish Your Soul

A *little bit every day* can do great good for your soul.

I read the Bible to my kids during breakfast. I don't read a lot. Maybe just a few verses. But I work hard to do it every weekday.

My wife and I pray for one of our children, a different child each night, before we go to bed. We usually take just a few minutes. We don't pray lengthy, expansive prayers. Usually we're brief and to the point. But we try to do this most every night.

What do you see in these examples? Although they don't take long, these practices are edifying, hopeful, and effective.

This devotional is just the same. Each entry is short—just a few tasty morsels of Scripture to nourish your hungry soul. Add it to your daily Bible reading. Read it on the subway or the bus on your way to work. Read it with a friend or a spouse every night at dinner. Make it part of each day for thirty-one days, and it will do you great good.

Why is that?

We start with Scripture. God's Word is powerful. Used by the Holy Spirit, it turns the hearts of kings, brings comfort to the lowly, and gives spiritual sight to the blind. It transforms lives and turns them upside down. We know that the Bible is God's very own words, so we read and study it to know God Himself.

Our study of Scripture is practical. Theology should change how we live. It's crucial to connect the Word with your daily life. Often, as you read this devotional, you'll see the word *you* because Lou speaks directly to you, the reader. Each reading usually contains at least one reflection question and practical suggestion. You'll get much more from this experience if you answer Lou's questions and do the practical exercises. Don't skip them. Do them for the sake of your own soul.

Our study of Scripture is worshipful. Maybe you are frustrated (even angry) with yourself because you've not lived up to your own high standards this week. Maybe you are far too often displeased with aspects of yourself that are not displeasing to God. Maybe you don't know what to do because God has thrown an obstacle in the way of what you want to accomplish. Or you've been avoiding certain people or situations out of fear of rejection. If you look around your life, you'll find signs of perfectionism everywhere. That's why God's Word matters. As a sinner, you are an imperfect person who is striving after unrealistic or unhealthy self-imposed standards. You can't fight this battle on your own. You need a Savior who is merciful, long-suffering, and patient with you. He in turn will lead you to be grateful for Him. What should your study of God's Word lead you to do? Worship Him. Every time you feel trapped by your perfectionism, it should remind you to say, "I can't do this on my own. I need Jesus to help me." You need a Savior who can rescue you from your sin and change you—not just one time but daily. As you study your Bible, you will learn that God has a lot to say about perfectionism, and He will help you to fight it.

If you find this devotional helpful (and I trust that you will!), reread it in different seasons of your life. Whenever you have to fight your perfectionism, it will remind you of God's goodness and power and promises. Work through it this coming month, and then come back to it a year from now to remind yourself about what God and the gospel teach us about cultivating lives free of perfectionism.

This devotional starts you on a wonderful journey in which you'll grow in Christ. After you finish reading (and rereading) it, if you want more, you'll see more resources listed at the end of the book. Buy them and make good use of them.

Are you ready? Let's begin.

Deepak Reju

INTRODUCTION

Just Stop It?

"Relax!"

"Stop trying so hard!"

"Don't be so idealistic."

"Cut yourself some slack."

"You can't be the best at everything."

"Nobody's perfect."

"It's not that big of a deal!"

"You need to take a chill pill."

If you're reading this daily devotional, chances are you've heard sentiments like these from people who have noticed your determination to accomplish a task—or your frustration over not being able to accomplish a task according to your own specifications. In your heart, you know they're probably at least partly right. But you also know that you cannot simply *stop* your perfectionistic tendencies the way you might turn off a ceiling fan with a wall switch. You've been thinking this way for as long as you can remember. These thought patterns are deeply engraved in your mind—they are a part of who you are as a person and how you make dozens of decisions every day. Furthermore, you don't really want to change them—well, at least not all of them. "I never want to stop trying to be the best. It just wouldn't be me."

Forgive me for saying this, but please relax for a moment. I am not going to suggest that you become someone other than the person God made you to be. If the Lord intended you to be a John or a Susan, He is not planning on turning you into a Jimmy or a Stella—He just wants you to be the John or Susan whom He intended you to be.

And, as far as simply stopping your perfectionism on command, that's not the solution. A battleship cannot turn on a dime but must reorient itself in a new direction over the course of many meters—especially if the new orientation is a complete 180-degree turn. So think of this little book as a resource that will, little by little, help you to navigate your heart in a new direction.

"But wait a minute, Lou! I think you are forgetting something! There are a number of Scripture passages that seem to compel me to, in fact, be perfect (see Matt. 5:48), to excel even beyond what I am already doing (see 1 Thess. 4:10), and to diligently strive after certain things (see 2 Peter 1:5–7). How can I stop trying to be perfect when the Bible requires me to pursue excellence? My conscience may not allow me to 'relax' quite as easily as you say."

Great point! But have you considered that your conscience may have to be reprogrammed? That is, it may have to be purged of extrabiblical rules and fortified with a proper, more theologically accurate understanding of the passages that have previously impelled you to undertake an inordinate pursuit of excellence. Mature (or "perfect") Christians train their consciences to increasingly align with the Word of God: "Solid food is for the mature, for those who have their powers of discernment trained by constant practice to distinguish good from evil" (Heb. 5:14 ESV).

Reading and applying this book will largely be an exercise in retraining your conscience to know the difference between what a sin really is and is not and to know when trying to do a good thing becomes a bad thing in God's eyes.

Please keep in mind that perfectionism is an issue that is not identified by name in the Bible—at least not by this name. But because it is one of those temptations that is "common to man" (1 Cor. 10:13), Scripture both identifies its underlying sinful roots[1] and prescribes its solutions. There is hope and help on the pages that follow. As a biblical counselor for over thirty-seven years, I've had the privilege of helping many who struggle with these tendencies (including at least one member of my immediate family) to find freedom in Christ from the bondage and misery so often associated with this unbiblical mindset.

Although I do not struggle with all-or-nothing thinking as a rule, there are certain areas in my life in which I do battle "perfectionism." For example, I sometimes take longer than I should to make decisions because I want to be sure I have considered every biblical directive and principle before I set the decision in concrete. My wife and daughter reminded me yesterday that I am also perfectionistic (I prefer the word *persnickety*) about my food. My pasta must be done al dente, my coffee (which must be imported from Italy) and my soup must be piping hot (vichyssoise excepted), my cheese served at room temperature, my Coke poured into a glass filled with ice, my eggs runny, my meat medium rare, my fish sizzling but moist, my cooked vegetables more crunchy than soggy, my fried food salted and served immediately, and my ice cream not too sweet and not too cold. It's not difficult to see what I value simply by looking at my struggles in this area.

What about you? What perfectionistic tendencies do you struggle with? Are you a perfectionist or simply a person who pursues excellence in certain areas? To what extent is your desire to excel rooted in your love for the Lord? To what extent might it be grounded in the love of people's approval or some other idolatrous desire? What do you overvalue?

To answer these questions, you need to have a clear understanding of what perfectionism is. Over the course of this devotional, I will give you several biblical working definitions of perfectionism. These should serve as guiding principles to help you to grow out of your perfectionism and enable you to make wiser choices in the future than you have in the past.

"Okay, but I have one more question. I really like my perfectionistic tendencies and don't want to change. I mean, sure, there is some daily misery associated with being a perfectionist, but I don't mind tolerating a little misery. I'm not sure I want to do all the work of changing unless my perfectionism really is a sin and God really does want me to change."

I agree. Why invest time, effort, and thought into changing something that doesn't need to be changed—especially when there are so many more apparent sin issues that God wants us to work on? You and I will probably not change unless we are convinced that God requires us to do so.

I believe the manifold sinfulness of perfectionism will become apparent as you read through this devotional. But for now, consider what is the most common sinful motivation of perfectionists. (Hint: it is, arguably, the most serious sin in the Bible—one that God promises to judge quickly and severely.) Is it not the sin of pride? In one way or another, perfectionists are more concerned about establishing their own reputation (and agenda) than God's. Their striving after flawlessness belies the fact that they are fallen creatures who will never be perfect in this life. In other words, such people may think more highly of themselves than they ought. Moreover, it is pride that tempts them to compare themselves with others and spend inordinate amounts of time on tasks that will demonstrate their superiority to others. As you work through the manifestations of perfectionism described in this book, see if you can connect the dots between each of them and the sin of pride.

"This sounds at least mildly painful. You want me to face up to my pride, and you probably want me to change. I don't think I can do that! The way I've lived my life is too deeply ingrained."

This is not something you can do on your own, but with God's help, you can change. As you read this devotional, remember all that God has done for you already. He sent His Son to live a perfect life for your sake and then to atone for all your sin by His death. Now Christ lives again, and He offers you a new way to live—a way that is empowered by His Spirit (see John 14:26) and His Word (see Isa. 55:10–11). Not only that, He's given you spiritual leaders and a spiritual family to come alongside you and help you to bear your burdens (see Gal. 6:2; Eph. 4:11–16;). If you are willing to face your pride of perfectionism and look for a different way to live, there is hope.

DAY 1

Union with Christ

We were buried with Him through baptism into death, so that as Christ was raised from the dead through the glory of the Father, so we too might walk in newness of life. For if we have become united with Him in the likeness of His death, certainly we shall also be in the likeness of His resurrection. (Rom. 6:4–5)

OUR UNION WITH CHRIST is one of the most essential doctrines for Christian living. Yet sadly it is also one of the most neglected, under-taught, and undervalued, resulting in many problems in the lives of believers.

Do you understand what your union with Christ means? Matt Fuller has a helpful analogy: "When you become a Christian, you're united by faith to Jesus. His story becomes yours. . . . Imagine a baby inside a mother's womb. The baby's life is determined by what mum does. If she dives to the bottom of a swimming pool, then so does the baby. If she takes [an elevator] to the top of a skyscraper, so does the baby. If the mother eats hot spicy food, the baby even knows about that! The child is united to its mother, and dependent upon its mother for life, and whatever mum experiences, so does the child."[1]

Let's consider our text for today. It says that through baptism, you have been buried with Christ into death. To be baptized into His death is to be baptized into His resurrection. What happened to Christ has happened to you as well. Why? Because, like a baby in his or her mother's womb, you are now in Him. He died, so you died. He was resurrected, so you are resurrected. He lives, so you live.

Understanding this principle will completely transform how you view your sanctification—the lifelong, Spirit-driven process by which you are freed from sin and made holy. Paul also tells us, "Our old man was crucified with Him, in order that our body of sin might be done away with, so that we would no longer be slaves to sin" (Rom. 6:6). This means that, as a result of being united to Christ, you have died to your old, sinful way of living and will now live in a new and different way.[2]

"What does this have to do with perfectionistic, all-or-nothing thinking?" you ask.

A lot more than I can put in this small book! Everything that follows will make sense if you grasp this concept. But how about this for today's takeaway? You have been fused to a person who is truly perfect. Nothing you can do will improve upon His perfection. Will you embrace and rejoice in His perfection, or will you continue to try to establish your own? Do you want others to see and marvel at your flawed attempts at perfection or at His total perfection?

Reflect: In what specific ways has your union with Christ changed how you live? What perfectionistic thought patterns can you identify that ought to change in light of this union?

Act: Write down in your own words how you would explain your union with Christ to a friend.

DAY 2

Are You a Perfectionist?

Let us test and examine our ways, and return to the LORD*! (Lam. 3:40 ESV)*

IF WE WANT to find God's solution to our problem, it is important that we understand our problem as God does—through the lens of Scripture. He gave us His Word to correct us and train us in righteousness (see 2 Tim. 3:16). Today's text says we must not only examine ourselves but also return to the Lord and His way of doing things. The Hebrew word for *return* in the verse is the one most commonly used in the Old Testament to mean *repent*. The idea is to *turn back*: when we realize we are going in the wrong direction, we turn around and go back in the right direction.

So, how about a few self-examination questions to help you to evaluate if you need to turn back from perfectionistic thinking? How often are the following statements true of you?

- I find it difficult to disclose who I really am to those closest to me.
- My family, friends, or coworkers would say that I am too demanding of them or that I have unrealistic expectations of them.
- I procrastinate because I'm afraid that I'll not be able to perform perfectly.
- I beat myself up when I make a mistake; making a mistake is terrible to me.
- I believe if I don't always give 100 percent, I'm being irresponsible.
- I'm afraid of failure.
- I have an all-or-nothing mentality. If I can't have it all, I don't want any of it.

- I have difficulty distinguishing what God considers to be unacceptable behavior from what my friends and family consider to be unacceptable behavior.
- I find it hard to relax when there is more work to be done.
- I believe that once I've started a task, I've got to finish it.
- I believe in following rules to the letter.
- I evaluate myself more on the basis of external attributes, such as personal achievements and productivity, than on the basis of Christlike character.
- When I sin publicly, I'm much more troubled because I have embarrassed myself than because I have embarrassed God.
- I avoid depending on others because I don't want to expose them to my own limitations.
- I evaluate myself on how I compare to others instead of comparing my work to how the Bible calls me to perform.

Don't be discouraged if you answered "frequently" or "almost always" to many of these questions. Perfectionism is an unbiblical mindset, but be of good cheer: Jesus Christ came to do away with your sin!

Reflect: Pick three statements from today's list that most indicate your perfectionistic tendencies. List them in order of significance.

Act: Show the list to three people who know you well and ask them for their input.

DAY 3

What Is Perfectionism?

The creation was subjected to futility, not willingly, but because of him who subjected it, in hope that the creation itself will be set free from its bondage to corruption and obtain the freedom of the glory of the children of God. (Rom. 8:20–21 ESV)

PERHAPS YOU'VE HEARD a perfectionist humorously described as "someone who takes great pains and gives them to others." Today let's look at a biblical definition of perfectionism: *perfectionism is expecting God to give me in this life what He has promised to give me only in the next.* Perfectionists want to live in a world without sin, sickness, suffering, and Satan. The problem is, except for the first and last two chapters of the Bible, we find at least one of these four *S*s on every page. It is not until the *next* life that those of us who know Christ as our Savior and Lord will be free of them.

Have you come to grips with this reality? Or are you frustrated with God for forcing you to live in a corrupted environment? Because of the fall, we live no longer in the garden of Eden but in a world bereaved of its splendor. Perhaps you understand this on an intellectual basis, but do you live your life as though it is true?

Our passage reminds us that, as a part of God's creation, we have been involuntarily subjected to futility. The world in which we live is broken and full of misery. Apart from Christ, and our belief in the new heavens and new earth, our world is a pretty miserable place to live. But Christians don't live "under the sun," as Solomon repeatedly declares in Ecclesiastes—we live "under the Son." We live not for this life or for this world but for the world and the life that are to come.

The first step in learning to overcome your perfectionistic tendencies may be for you to reevaluate your thinking about the world in which God has placed you. You are living not in paradise but on a battlefield to which He has drafted you to serve as His soldier. To strive for perfection now is an exercise in futility.

Yesterday, we looked at the primary Old Testament word for *repent*. Today, I would like you to consider the New Testament Greek word for *repentance*. It is a compound word that combines a word for *think* with a word for *again*. In Greek, to repent means to "think again" or to "rethink" something.

To have any hope of losing your perfectionistic tendencies, you must change how you think and how you interpret the world in which you live. You will have to learn to think biblically about all of God's creation—including yourself. And you will have to reset your affections from this life to the next one.

As you go through your upcoming day, why not meditate on specific ways you can begin to adjust your thoughts, motives, and especially your values in order to gain an eternal perspective on living as a fallen creature in a fallen world? Then give some thought to what it will be like to be free from sin, sickness, suffering, and Satan when the Lord Jesus Christ reveals His glory in you.

Reflect: What exactly do you have to rethink and reinterpret about living in a world that has been cursed by sin?

Act: Spend five or ten minutes today thinking about what it will be like to live in a world without sin, sickness, suffering, and Satan.

DAY 4

What Perfectionism Is Not

"Therefore you are to be perfect, as your heavenly Father is perfect." (Matt. 5:48)

TODAY'S VERSE IS perplexing. Is Jesus really commanding us to do something that is humanly unattainable in this life? Only God is perfect and without sin. Does Jesus want us to strive for perfection in this life *as if* it were attainable, knowing we will never succeed until the next? Or does He want us to realize that seeking perfection apart from His righteousness is an exercise in futility? Is this command designed to drive us to trust in His perfection, which has been imputed to our account?

I think something else is happening here. The Greek word translated *perfect* has several meanings. It can mean "complete," "mature," "fully grown," "whole," "without blemish," and "blameless." The verses that precede our text for today give us a clue for understanding it. In those verses, Jesus tells His listeners to go beyond loving their friends and siblings, which even the Gentiles do, and to love their enemies. In this way, they can show that they are "sons of your Father who is in heaven. For he makes his sun rise on the evil and on the good, and sends rain on the just and on the unjust" (Matt. 5:45 ESV).

God goes beyond what man naturally does. He loves not only those who love Him but those who hate Him. He loves His enemies. We are to do likewise. We are to love others *perfectly*—not in the sense of *flawlessly* but in the sense of *going beyond what others do* in the way God does. He does not hold back as others might in similar circumstances. He wants us to grow up and mature into His way of loving. God doesn't confine His love only to good people.[1] He doesn't hold back but goes beyond what others might do by loving His enemies. He gives 100 percent.

Jesus's command to be perfect in light of God's perfection is not about doing everything perfectly. It is about faithfulness, not flawlessness. It's about making progress toward Christlikeness, not about pursuing perfection. The Greek tense of the verb *to be perfect* has an eye toward the future. And although it has the force of an injunction, technically it is not an imperative. It might be rendered as "You shall perfect yourself" or perhaps "You will be perfected."

It is the goal that we aim for. We lay aside every weight and sin that clings to us, running with endurance the race that is set before us as we set our eyes on the author and perfecter of our faith (see Heb. 12:1–2). *Jesus* is the author of your faith. Not you. *Jesus* is the perfecter of your faith, not you. Yes, you must cooperate with Him, but He is the one who is doing the work in you.

Whether you strive or give up, you are a failure as long as you are faithless. Though you might not yet be a success, the moment you trust in God to change you, you are no longer a failure—you are in the process of being made perfect. As you heed and obey Christ's teachings, equipped by His Holy Spirit, you are on your way to becoming more mature, whole, and blameless.

Reflect: How have you progressed in your ability to love people around you who are difficult to love? Would learning to love difficult people make it easier for you to get your focus off yourself? Why?

Act: List the three people you find most difficult to love. For each one, identify what you believe are their three greatest needs. Evaluate the resources that God has given you and see how you may be able to use those resources to meet their needs.

DAY 5

Conforming Your Thoughts to Reality

Finally, brothers and sisters, whatever is true, whatever is honorable, whatever is just, whatever is pure, whatever is lovely, whatever is commendable, if there is any excellence, if there is anything worthy of praise, think about these things. (Phil. 4:8 ESV)

TODAY I WOULD like to focus your attention on the phrase "whatever is true." As a Christian, you are to think about things that *conform to reality*. If you are expecting God to pluck you out of this sin-cursed world and transport you prematurely into a world without sin, sickness, suffering, and Satan, you are not living in biblical reality. You may be thinking and living according to an unattainable fantasy.

That's right! Perfectionists live in a kind of fantasyland in which they and those around them are, or should be, capable of limitless feats. They may see themselves as superheroes with herculean qualities. They may spend inordinate amounts of time and effort trying to prove that they are capable of doing more than most others. Perhaps the worst part about it is that they take the credit for the abilities that they have been given, forgetting that any success is the direct result of God's grace and mercy (see 1 Cor. 4:7; James 1:17).

Here are some examples of these kinds of unrealistic, fanciful expectations:

- I will (or should) get to the point where I will be able to totally control my emotions.
- My spouse will eventually understand me completely and never be provoked by my idiosyncrasies.
- My house will be company-ready at all times.

- I will never get anything less than an A on tests and assignments.
- My children will cheerfully obey me at all times.
- I shouldn't have to tolerate people around me who mess up.
- I will flawlessly accomplish my work, activities, and tasks.
- I must always finish everything I have started.
- I should not be interrupted from my tasks.
- I must never fail.

Do you see how this kind of thinking denies the reality of an imperfect world? In a sin-cursed world, it is not possible to have a company-ready house 24/7. Living after the fall, you cannot expect to never blow a test, to never have a low-efficiency day at the office, or to never have to abort a project you've started. In God's reality, you won't necessarily have super compliant children or a spouse or a boss who is always reasonable. Expecting others to not mess up, make mistakes, or fail does not conform to reality either—nor does expecting yourself to succeed at everything you attempt. Otherwise, you would no longer need a Savior, would you?

Why not stop right now and confess to God any distorted view about yourself or others that you have identified today. Thank Him for covering your "imperfections" with the blood of Christ. Ask Him for the wisdom and grace to interpret life through the lens of Scripture.

Reflect: What are the three most unrealistic expectations you have for yourself—expectations that do not conform to the reality of living in a sin-cursed world?

Act: Memorize Philippians 4:8. Adjust the expectations identified above so that they accurately reflect living in a world that is impacted by sin, sickness, suffering, and Satan.

DAY 6

Enjoying Your Labor

Behold, what I have seen to be good and fitting is to eat and drink and find enjoyment in all the toil with which one toils under the sun the few days of his life that God has given him, for this is his lot. Everyone also to whom God has given wealth and possessions and power to enjoy them, and to accept his lot and rejoice in his toil—this is the gift of God. (Eccl. 5:18–19 ESV)

Perfectionism is striving after accomplishments more than faithfulness. Today we'll focus on the first part of this second working definition of perfectionism that we have drawn from Scripture—striving after accomplishment.

God designed us to work, to eat, to drink, and to enjoy whatever good we receive through our labor. This is our divinely appointed earthly portion. As Paul puts it, we deal with the world without becoming totally absorbed in it (see 1 Cor. 7:31). In our verses for today, we see that Solomon "wants us *to freely enjoy* what God graciously allows us to earn—so long as we do not hoard, do not withhold from those in need, and do not make wealth our ambition in life out of love for money."[1]

Because of the fall, a certain amount of misery now accompanies our toil. Yet the enjoyment we find in that labor is God's gift to us. This means it's not wrong for us to seek pleasure in, and even look forward to, the earnings of our labor *and also* the sense of achievement we have regarding the things we do.

That said, perfectionistic people often do sin in how they enjoy their accomplishments. How? By leaving God out of the equation.

As with any pleasurable activity or experience, it is idolatry to seek that sense of accomplishment as an end *in and of itself* rather than as a means to a greater end, such as thanking, glorifying, or otherwise worshipping God. In other words, it is very appropriate to use your sense of accomplishment as a springboard to worship God. He is the one who gave you the ability to achieve each gratifying undertaking. But when you focus on the accomplishment itself and the personal satisfaction it brings you, without fixing your gaze upon God and His purposes for your toil, you are delighting more in your pleasure than in God who gave you the pleasure.

For many perfectionists, *love of achievement* is their hearts' idol. Their desire for achievement may or may not be consciously attached to the love of people's approval—some people love to have achieved something whether others notice it or not. In either case, to experience this pleasure apart from the Lord is to distort God's purposes for that pleasure.

Reflect: Think of a time when you prioritized achievement over obeying, trusting, or loving God. Do you think achievement is an idol for you? Why or why not?

Act: List three ways you can use your achievements as springboards to worship God. Practice right now. Thank God for the things He has allowed you to accomplish this past week. Ask God to help you bring Him into your future experiences of accomplishment.

DAY 7

On Pursuing Excellence

Now concerning love of the brothers, you have no need for anyone to write to you, for you yourselves are taught by God to love one another. . . . But we urge you, brothers, to excel still more. (1 Thess. 4:9–10)

TODAY'S PASSAGE HAS caused me some confusion, even a bit of frustration, over the past few years. If Paul commends the Thessalonians for loving one another—saying God Himself has taught them love—why does he tell them to excel even more? Is he not satisfied with their progress? On day 4, we saw that Jesus wants us to pursue faithfulness, not flawlessness. Is Paul arguing for something different? Talk about a perfectionist!

Love is the greatest commandment. Yes, the Thessalonians didn't need anyone to teach them *how* to love. They knew how to love, and for that they were commended. But they did need *to grow* in their ability to love one another. You and I are flawed, and we will be so until the Lord returns. Until then, Scripture frequently exhorts us to grow up into Christ. To want to excel in *Christlikeness* is not necessarily perfectionistic. To want to excel at excellence often is.

Consider someone who says, "I'm going to be the best I can be in whatever I decide is important, irrespective of what matters most to God." Such a person is pursuing excellence for the sake of excellence. This, however, is not a biblical goal.

Is it wrong to be an excellent athlete or musician or accountant? That depends on your motive. If you are diligently seeking the things the Bible says you should be seeking (like Christlike character) and are seeking excellence in other areas for the glory of God and the benefit of your neighbor, certainly it is not wrong. "Do you see a man skilled in his work? He will stand before kings;

He will not stand before obscure men" (Prov. 22:29). To diligently pursue a good thing for the right reasons is proper. But to separate "excellence" from a good thing and make it a virtue in and of itself misses the mark and leads to perfectionism.

Reflect: Are you pursuing excellence independently of those things the Bible says are necessary for Christlikeness? Are you spending so much time pursuing excellence in areas of your own choosing that you are neglecting pursuing excellence in areas that matter most to God?

Act: Make a list of the top five things that you are or have been diligently pursuing. Then ask yourself how these things might reflect godly character.

DAY 8

Perfection or Being Faithful

But the fruit of the Spirit is love, joy, peace, patience, kindness, goodness, faithfulness, gentleness, self-control; against such things there is no law. (Gal. 5:22–23 ESV)

HOW DO WE measure success? If striving to be perfect is not our goal, then what is? What's the biblical target we should set our sights on?

How about faithfulness? Remember the definition of perfectionism from a few days ago: it is striving after accomplishments more than faithfulness.

Over and over again, Scripture holds up faithfulness as a virtue. Indeed, as today's passage tells us, it is a fruit of the Spirit. But what is faithfulness? Faithfulness is demonstrating to God and others that you can be trusted. To be biblically faithful means that you are *dependable, reliable,* and *trustworthy*. It means that your yes always means yes and your no always means no. Faithful people understand their biblical responsibilities and don't allow other, less important things to distract them from doing what they have agreed to do.[1]

Perfectionists typically do not populate this category. Here's why. If you are striving to be perfect on each project, you will fail in other areas—most likely in areas that are more important to God than the ones on which you're trying to make a perfect score.

Consider your God-given week. God has supplied you with 168 hours and certain responsibilities that He wants you to fulfill during that time. You may have ancillary tasks that you want (or, for whatever reason, choose) to do.

When you try to squeeze too many tasks into your week, you will often find that you fail to accomplish the things that God wants you to do. If you're perfectionistic, the problem is likely not that you have assumed too many responsibilities but rather that you are spending too much time trying to get things to be perfect. Rather than spending a few hours on a particular task and being content with an A- (or, heaven forbid, a B+), you may spend countless hours on that project because getting the A+ is more important to you than fulfilling other God-given responsibilities. Consequently, at the end of the day (or week), you may have failed to do some of the things God's Word says you ought to have done, such as spending time in the Word, fellowshipping with other Christians, or ministering to your spouse and children.

If this describes you, the best thing you can do now is to choose to be faithful with the Lord's time. Punch the clock for whatever amount of time a task should reasonably take to eliminate the risk of failing to carry out the responsibilities God has given you. This may involve a paradigm shift in your thinking. Namely, rather than thinking in terms of perfectly completing one project at a time, it might be better for you to think in terms of time (minutes, hours, and days) per project in light of all your biblical responsibilities.

Reflect: What biblical responsibilities have you been failing to do in your attempt to get a perfect score in tasks for which God doesn't require perfection?

Act: Identify the top two responsibilities you are spending more time on than you can biblically justify and assign them a new time limit.

DAY 9

Displeasure

Woe to those who call evil good and good evil, who put darkness for light and light for darkness, who put bitter for sweet and sweet for bitter! (Isa. 5:20 ESV)

To call something evil that God has called good is a serious problem! It's one thing to set a standard *for yourself* that is higher than God's. But to condemn yourself for not achieving your self-imposed higher standard is to call something that is proper (good) improper (evil). It is not only to judge yourself sinfully but also to judge the Bible and its Author to be in error (see James 4:11–12).

One of the effects of raising the bar higher than God's standard as found in Scripture is that we are displeased with ourselves in areas where God is not. This gives us another definition for perfectionism: *the tendency to be displeased with myself about things that aren't displeasing to God.* This can produce in us unbiblical inferiority judgments—we may develop a thought pattern in which we judge ourselves to be inferior in areas that God does not view as problematic, sinful, or even abnormal. To the degree that we are committed to perfecting these unbiblical "imperfections," we lose focus on collaborating with the Holy Spirit to correct the actual sin in our lives. We also reinforce a temporal value system by "correcting" things that will not matter in eternity.

What is the meaning of the phrase "who put darkness for light and light for darkness, who put bitter for sweet and sweet for bitter"?

Darkness has to do with error or false doctrine. Light is emblematic of truth—anything that conforms to reality. To set your mind on the things of man rather than the things of God is to err: it is, in a sense, to accept and believe false doctrine. We don't often think in these terms, but at the end of the day, believing false doctrine is a sin—and sin produces misery!

To put bitter for sweet is to choose the misery associated with sin—unbiblical thinking, in the case of the perfectionist—over the pleasure of learning to think biblically. We ought to value the things of God more than the things of man. By God's grace, you can learn how to prefer good over evil, to prefer light over darkness, and to choose sweet over bitter.

Reflect: What temporal things are you inordinately setting your mind on? What eternal things ought you to be setting your mind on?

Act: List the top five miseries associated with your perfectionistic pursuit of temporal things. List the top five blessings that you might experience if you dethrone your idolatrous desire for perfection.

Act: Identify a trusted Christian friend to whom you can confess your idolatrous desires for perfectionism. While confession is scary, coming into the light is honoring to God and good for your soul.

DAY 10

At Least

"But his master answered him, 'You wicked and slothful servant! You knew that I reap where I have not sown and gather where I scattered no seed? Then you ought to have invested my money with the bankers, and at my coming I should have received what was my own with interest.'" (Matt. 25:26–27 ESV)

THE WORDS *AT LEAST* do not appear in the Greek text of this passage, but they are implicit. "You ought to have [at least] invested my money with the bankers, and at my coming I should have received what was my own with interest." The master had left money with his servants when he went on a journey. He did not require a doubling or tripling of his investment but would have been satisfied with interest. Instead, his servant did nothing. One wonders if he would have preferred a small loss to that!

Perfectionists tend to have an all-or-nothing mindset. "Anything less than an A+ might as well be an F, so I'm not going to try." "If I don't spend at least an hour in my quiet time, I basically didn't have one." "Since I didn't stick to my eating plan today, it proves I have no self-control, so I'm done trying to eat healthily." "If my children misbehave, clearly I'm a terrible parent."

But is this the way we should think? Do these kinds of thoughts conform to reality? Are they consistent with how God thinks about our achievements?

God gives each of us our own different responsibilities and different measures of ability. Some of us are able to get more done in our allotted time than others can. Each of the servants in Jesus's parable was given talents "according to his own ability" (Matt. 25:15). Our Master knows better than we do what our capacities are; therefore, He knows that we are all capable of different levels of accomplishment.

God has given you specific talents, abilities, skills, and interests. He knows what you are able to do with what He has given you. His expectations are largely based on the assets He has provided you. His expectations are not exactly the same for every person. He doesn't, for example, expect every baseball player to have the same batting average or hit the same number of home runs. Neither does He expect every singer to have the same vocal range. He is content with far less than perfection—far less than what people who foolishly compare themselves to others expect of themselves. He will not demand of you that which you are incapable of doing, but He does expect you to faithfully use the things He has given you for His glory. And that brings us to the issue with many perfectionists. Perfectionists are often interested in promoting their own kingdom and glory rather than the Lord's.

How about you? Is it hard for you to be content with "at least"? Can you take comfort in the thought "Maybe it wasn't perfect, but at least I accomplished something"? If the thought of mediocrity, in light of your divinely selected limitations of time, total responsibilities, and gifts, is unbearable, you are likely not savoring the things of God but of man. May I suggest that you ask yourself, "Am I still trying to please people, or am I trying to please God?" (see Gal. 1:10).[1]

Reflect: What are your most common perfectionistic all-or-nothing kinds of thoughts?

Act: Make a list of the areas in which you should consider lowering your expectations from perfection to "at least."

DAY 11

Weaknesses

But he said to me, "My grace is sufficient for you, for my power is made perfect in weakness." Therefore I will boast all the more gladly of my weaknesses, so that the power of Christ may rest upon me. For the sake of Christ, then, I am content with weaknesses, insults, hardships, persecutions, and calamities. For when I am weak, then I am strong. (2 Cor. 12:9–10 ESV)

ARE YOU AFRAID of being seen as weak? The apostle Paul wasn't.

"But doesn't he repeatedly encourage us to be strong? Didn't he pray that we would be?"

He did. But did he want us to be strong by our own power or, as Peter put it, "by the strength which God supplies" (1 Peter 4:11)?

In our passage for today, Paul, having asked the Lord three times to remove his thorn in the flesh and being told no, decided to allow the Lord to pour out His supernatural help on him. Isn't it interesting that God uses the word *perfect* here? It is God's *perfect* power that He wants to display in Paul's weakness.

Have you ever been stuck by a thorn? Can you imagine having a thorn embedded under your skin or in a muscle? Whatever Paul's thorn in the flesh was, it was painful. He wanted it gone. What kind of pain did his thorn produce? It may very well have been something that was embarrassing to him—or perhaps embarrassing to his ministry. It was, after all, given to him so that he would not exalt himself (see 2 Cor. 12:7).

Yet not only does Paul *gladly* boast of his weaknesses so that Christ's power will descend and remain on him, but he takes pleasure in it. The word *content* means that he considers his weakness to be a good thing.

Is that how it is with you? Are you content with your non-sinful imperfections? Are you willing to be seen as less than perfect so that God's perfect power will be manifested to all who know about your imperfections? Are you willing to gladly boast about your weaknesses so that God will be glorified, even if it means you may be temporarily embarrassed? Humbling yourself by displaying some of your imperfections to certain people might be the single best remedy for your perfectionism. God resists the proud but gives grace to the humble (see James 4:6; 1 Peter 5:5).

As one of my favorite commentators put it, "It is when man is consciously weak that this power becomes most fully manifest to the human consciousness and takes most precious effect in sustaining the otherwise sinking soul. . . . The more my own strength seems to go out of me, the more conscious shall I become of being filled with Christ. This is [the] Christian experience."[1]

May God help you take your efforts to perfect your weaknesses and replace them with the desire to have Christ's strength be manifested through them.

Reflect: What are the three areas in which you are most afraid of being seen as weak or imperfect?

Act: Try to identify five ways God could be glorified by demonstrating His strength in or through each of the weaknesses identified above. List three ways you could actually boast in these weaknesses. If you are willing, share your insights with a trusted Christian friend.

DAY 12

Sober-Mindedness

For by the grace given to me I say to everyone among you not to think of himself more highly than he ought to think, but to think with sober judgment, each according to the measure of faith that God has assigned. (Rom. 12:3 ESV)

FOR THE NEXT few days, we'll consider our next working definition: *perfectionism is the inordinate desire to be, or appear to be, better than I am realistically capable of being.*

Today's passage urges us to not think more highly of ourselves than is proper but rather to soberly assess ourselves in light of the faith God has sovereignly measured out to us. "God, in accordance with His sovereign purposes, *distributed to each* Christian *a measure of faith* (i.e., a portion fitting to his faith as a gift of the Spirit). [Each Christian] must discover what his gifts are and be satisfied with them."[1]

Faith is the doorway through which enter all the other graces and gifts that God bestows on us. At the end of the day, it is God who gives us the ability to do whatever we do (see also 1 Cor. 4:7). But many get tripped up in dissatisfaction with God's distribution of gifts. Perfectionists often exaggerate their strengths and minimize or ignore their weaknesses. They overestimate their gifts, their abilities, their opinions, and even their contributions to the body of Christ way beyond what a sober-minded, truthful evaluation would allow. They tend to operate under the assumption that they, rather than God, are ultimately responsible for their achievements and success. What is at the core of this self-aggrandizement? Often it is a desire to be better or be seen as better in certain areas than they are realistically capable of being.

To be sure, given enough time people can excel in any number of things, should they choose to do so. But is it realistic—or rational, as the Greek word for "sober judgment" implies—to invest so much time, effort, and thought in perfecting things that don't matter to God as much as they matter to you? And at what cost? And to the neglect of what other responsibilities?

Are you dissatisfied with the way God has chosen to gift you? If you were Him, would you have assigned yourself different—or greater—abilities, gifts, and talents? Rather than believing you know better than He does about such things, would it not be better to understand and perfect what He has given you?

Reflect: What gifts, abilities, and talents are you consciously trying to perfect right now? Do you believe your assessment of yourself in these areas is accurate? To whom can you talk to help you determine whether your assessments are correct?

Act: List the gifts and special abilities you believe God has given you. Determine how you have used each item on your list for building your own kingdom and reputation. Make a list of the ways you can use them, starting today, to build God's kingdom for His glory and the benefit of others.

DAY 13

All or Nothing

Be not overly righteous, and do not make yourself too wise. Why should you destroy yourself? Be not overly wicked, neither be a fool. Why should you die before your time? (Eccl. 7:16–17 ESV)

EARLY IN MY counseling ministry, I was helping a newspaper journalist. I was in the process of working on my first book, and when the counseling session was over, I asked him if he could give me some counsel about writing. I can't remember the exact question I asked him, but I will never forget his answer: "We have a saying at the office: *nothing is that good, and nothing is that bad.*"

In other words, no article is so good that someone on the staff can't make it better, and no article is so bad that a good editor can't make it fit to print. That, for me, has been one of the most freeing sayings—one that has helped me not only in authoring books but in many other areas of life. However, the mantra of a perfectionist is more along the lines of "almost everything is that bad, and hardly anything is any good."

Perfectionistic people struggle with all-or-nothing thinking. Everything is *absolutely* black or white, great or terrible, failure or success, miracle or catastrophe. In their minds, everything belongs in one of two categories: good or bad. There is no room in their thinking for the many shades of gray in God's creation. The thought that something good might have a tinge of bad in it, or that something bad might contain a fair amount of good, is foreign to them. But today's passage encourages us to avoid such extremes.[1]

Think, for a moment, about God's control over the weather. Right now, I'm sitting in a hotel lobby looking out the window. It's a cloudy, rainy, dark, and dreary day. But plenty of light is making its way through the clouds. Tomorrow is forecasted to be partly sunny. The next day, very sunny. God doesn't make every day 100 percent sunny or 100 percent dark.

At the end of the day, all-or-nothing thinking is a habit. It is a learned way of interpreting life that becomes locked in through frequent practice. But, for the follower of Jesus Christ, it can be changed. Over the next few days, we will look at some of the biblical remedies you can employ to rethink, or repent of, your all-or-nothing thinking.

Reflect: What areas of your life are you most likely to think about in a binary (all-or-nothing) way?

Act: Ask a trusted friend or family member to help you recall patterns of speech that you regularly use to express all-or-nothing, perfectionistic thinking (pessimistic outlooks, self-condemning phrases, sweeping generalizations such as *never, only*, or *always*).

DAY 14

Using Biblical Terminology

Now we have received, not the spirit of the world, but the Spirit who is from God, so that we may know the things freely given to us by God, which things we also speak, not in words taught by human wisdom, but in those taught by the Spirit, combining spiritual thoughts with spiritual words. (1 Cor. 2:12–13 NASB)

An important step in correcting disordered thinking is to label it according to its biblical name.[1] Using biblical terminology for such thinking is essential for at least two reasons. First, it reminds us that we are dealing with a sin that must be repented of, and this serves to convict us. Second, it makes it easier for us to locate passages in Scripture in which antidotes are found.

The term *perfectionism* isn't the most precise biblical term for the problem we're addressing. Depending on the nature of your thoughts and motives, more accurate wording might be *a focus on what is untrue, fear, anxiety, a tendency to make rash judgments or false prophecies, idolatry, pride, people-pleasing,* or *legalism* (teaching as doctrines the commandments of men). If you do use terms like *perfectionism* or *all-or-nothing thinking,* make sure you thoroughly understand the biblical nature of the patterns of thought into which you have fallen.

But regardless of what you call these kinds of thoughts, recognizing that you are having them and that they are unbiblical is essential to correcting them. I sometimes use the phrase "unpack and repack" when helping counselees to address all sorts of sinful thought patterns and motivations. "Let's unpack and repack what you are telling yourself," I might say. The *unpacking* usually begins with noticing the thought and identifying that it is, in fact, unbiblical. The second stage, *repacking,* is to label the various elements of the patterns in biblical terms.

Remember, the reason for identifying and categorizing your thinking in biblical terms is not to trigger another round of self-condemning thoughts. Don't allow yourself to go there. Rather, the purpose of this exercise is to take your thoughts captive (see 2 Cor. 10:5) and learn to speak truth in your heart (see Ps. 15:2) so that you may be totally transformed by the renewing of your mind (see Rom. 12:2). Remember also that if your perfectionistic thought patterns were primarily the result of genetics or biology, and were thus some type of medical issue, there would be little hope for a permanent cure. But if they are, in fact, the result of learned, sinful ways of interpreting and responding to your world, then you can learn to free yourself of them with God's help.

Reflect: What are the most common all-or-nothing things you tell yourself? Try to answer with the exact wording you typically use. Can you identify a common denominator to these thoughts?

Act: Identify in biblical terms the unbiblical nature of each thought.

DAY 15

Discerning Truth from Error

For the word of God is living and active, sharper than any two-edged sword, piercing to the division of soul and of spirit, of joints and of marrow, and discerning the thoughts and intentions of the heart. (Heb. 4:12 ESV)

PAUL TELLS US that we have received "the Spirit who is from God, that we might understand the things freely given us by God" (1 Cor. 2:12 ESV). When we open Scripture in faith, the Holy Spirit uses it to give us understanding and to supernaturally transform our hearts and lives from the inside out. Christ's Word and Spirit work to effectively replace our unbiblical, misery-producing ways of thinking with biblical, joyous ones.

Look at the last clause of today's passage. The word of God is, as the NASB renders it, "able to judge the thoughts and intentions of the heart." It puts your thoughts on trial. Apart from Scripture, it is impossible for us to accurately discern the nature and even the scope of our unbiblical thoughts and motives. We will never truly understand what we are dealing with, and as long as we do not understand, we cannot change.

If the first step in the process of correcting your perfectionistic thinking is to recognize when your thoughts are unbiblical, then the second step is to discover biblical replacements for those thoughts. You see, a Christian's process of change is not just about *breaking habits*—these habits must be *supplanted* with a biblical mindset and behavior. All through the Scriptures, we see this twofold process appear. Biblical counselors like to refer to it as the put-off / put-on dynamic. By faith and through the work of the Spirit, change is possible.

Yesterday I asked you to identify the most common all-or-nothing things you say to yourself. Today I'm going to ask you to search the Scriptures for godly alternatives to those thoughts. Ask the Holy Spirit to help you to answer the following questions.

What is the evidence that this thought is true?[1]

Is there any evidence to suggest it is untrue?[2]

What exactly is unbiblical about this thought? Is it *totally untrue* (an outright lie)? Is it *true but not totally true* (a distorted truth)? Is it *incomplete* (a truth that needs to be supplemented with another truth to render it more accurate)? Is it *lacking biblical hope* (a truth that needs to be supplemented with biblical hope to be biblically accurate)?

Remember the words of Paul: "It is my prayer that your love may abound more and more, with knowledge and all discernment" (Phil. 1:9 ESV). God has given you the tools that you need to grow in understanding and to live in the light of what Scripture teaches.

Reflect: Have you ever asked a trusted Christian friend or church leader to help you evaluate your thoughts in light of Scripture and reason? Who can you ask to help you put your thoughts on trial and cross-examine your perfectionistic ideations?

Reflect: No unpacking and repacking of thoughts happens successfully apart from faith in Christ (see Rom. 14:23). He is the one who gives spiritual insight (see 1 Cor. 2:12–13) and the ability to repent and change (see 2 Tim. 2:25). How might you be able to tell if your study of Scripture reflects humble faith?

Act: Using the appendix, see if you can correct and transform each perfectionistic thought you identify.

DAY 16

Infusing Your Thoughts with Hope

But this I call to mind, and therefore I have hope: The steadfast love of the L*ORD never ceases; his mercies never come to an end; they are new every morning; great is your faithfulness. "The* L*ORD is my portion," says my soul, "therefore I will hope in him."* (Lam. 3:21–24 ESV)

BECAUSE ALL-OR-NOTHING THINKERS, and other kinds of worriers, tend to emphasize the negative and omit the positive, their thought patterns bring them to despair. Today we'll work on infusing your thoughts with biblical hope.

Last year I came down with a pretty stiff case of COVID-19 that turned into pneumonia. After struggling for nine days, I found a facility that would give me a monoclonal antibody infusion. Within two days I felt much better.

Think, for a moment, that your perfectionistic thoughts are a virus that makes you weak and sick. Imagine being infused with the promises of God's Word. Now imagine what would happen if you regularly received an infusion of those promises. There is no more powerful prescription you can take to cure your perfectionistic thinking than God's Word. As Paul writes, "The word of God . . . *performs its work in you* who believe" (1 Thess. 2:13 NASB; see also Isa. 55:10–11).

In today's passage, in the depths of great depression and isolation, the prophet Jeremiah says something very interesting: "This I call to mind, and therefore I have hope." What breathed life into his depressing thoughts? His perspective changed when he thought of God's character. In a very real sense, the perfections of God—which we see most fully and clearly in the gospel of Christ—are promises that we can depend on Him. Rather than trying to save ourselves, we can embrace our Savior and rest in His goodness.

After lamenting over one thing or another, David and other psalmists found hope when they reminded themselves of God's character and His faithfulness to them in the past. As Christian explains to Hopeful in *The Pilgrim's Progress,* the promises of God are the keys that unlock every room in the dungeon. Perfectionistic thinking is a dungeon! May the Lord help you to learn how to shine the light of His promises in every room of the dungeon of your mind.

Reflect: To what extent would your thoughts (not just each one but the totality of your musings) benefit from an infusion of hope?

Reflect: Our hope is grounded in the cross. Christ died to redeem you from your unbiblical thoughts and disobedience. How ought that fact to change the way you approach your problems?

Act: When you next read a passage from the Psalms or the New Testament, look for and highlight specific promises that you can inject into your all-or-nothing interpretation of life, of yourself, and of the Lord.

DAY 17

Let the Word of Christ Dwell in You Richly

Let the word of Christ dwell in you richly, teaching and admonishing one another in all wisdom, singing psalms and hymns and spiritual songs, with thankfulness in your hearts to God. (Col. 3:16 ESV)

YESTERDAY, WE SAW that the promises of God, rooted in Christ, are an effective medication for all-or-nothing thinking. Today I would like to zoom out and look at the value of memorizing and meditating on the Word of God. This will help you take your medication in a way that transforms your life.

"*All Scripture* is breathed out by God and profitable for teaching, for reproof, for correction, and for training in righteousness" (2 Tim. 3:16 ESV). In this passage, Paul gives us four uses of Scripture. Notice the last two. The Scriptures are useful to *correct* our existing problems and to *train* us in righteousness. Scripture shows us how to replace unbiblical actions and thoughts with actions and thoughts that honor God.

Our text for today begins with the injunction "Let the word of Christ dwell in you richly." Jay Adams explains that this means Scripture ought to be "at home" in believers—not just an occasional guest. As it dwells in us, it becomes the "motivating and directing force in [our] living."[1]

Although reading Scripture makes a powerful impact, memorizing and meditating on appropriate portions of Scripture is even more powerful. First, find the passages that best relate to your specific disordered thought patterns. You may want to consider asking others, searching online, or using a study Bible or concordance to help you. Then, once you have identified and committed to memory the specific passages you would like to meditate on,

- personalize the passage by changing its pronouns to first-person singular;
- recite the passages to yourself repeatedly, emphasizing a different word or phrase each time;
- pray the passage back to the Lord;
- using sanctified imagination, picture how you can apply the passage as well as the temporal and eternal fruit that will be produced as a result of your application;
- try putting the passages to music and singing them to yourself;
- run the passage through 2 Timothy 3:16. How does it teach, reprove, correct, and train you?

As you explore the Scriptures for passages to memorize, look especially for passages that will call to mind the truth about Christ as your Lord, Savior, and Redeemer. Dwell on the gospel. Savor it in your thoughts and heart. Let it enrich your soul.

Reflect: How at home is the Word of God in your heart?

Act: Share some of the details of your struggle with perfectionistic thinking with several trusted, biblically literate friends or church leaders. Ask them to help you find specific passages of Scripture that relate to your style of perfectionistic thinking. Select the two passages that you believe will best address your all-or-nothing thinking.

DAY 18

On Beating Yourself Up

There is therefore now no condemnation for those who are in Christ Jesus. . . . Who shall bring any charge against God's elect? It is God who justifies. Who is to condemn? Christ Jesus is the one who died—more than that, who was raised—who is at the right hand of God, who indeed is interceding for us. (Rom. 8:1, 33–34 ESV)

I WOULD LIKE to begin today by focusing your attention on the word *no* in verse 1: "There is therefore now *no* condemnation for those who are in Christ Jesus." The word *no* is unequivocal! If you have been united to Christ, *nothing* and *no one* can rightfully condemn you. Not the law. Not the devil or his agents. Not other people. Not your own conscience. Not your self-condemning thoughts.

All such accusations are inadmissible evidence in the eyes of the Righteous Judge who has sent His Son to pay the penalty of our sins.

Let's look next at the first line of verse 33. Do you see the word *any*? "Who shall bring *any* charge against God's elect?" This is the other side of the same coin. If you are in Christ, no condemning charges will stick to you! Your Lawyer in heaven, who is seated at the right hand of God, interceding for you, quashes all indictments against you relating to your eternal standing and destiny.

Now, if this is the case, why do you take it on yourself to do the devil's work by beating yourself up over your imperfections? If your sins will not stick to you, how much less will your non-sinful imperfections! If you were before the bench in God's heavenly courtroom as the prosecuting attorney, do you really think you could say anything that would thwart the defense attorney's mission to suppress your charges?

"I know what you are saying is true, and that logically it's ridiculous for me to beat myself up with these thoughts, but I just can't seem to stop!"

Believe me, I understand. But maybe it would help if you set your mind on "things above" (Col. 3:1), in the sense of seeing your Advocate come to the defense of the person you are condemning (yourself). Hear Him laying out His case against the false accusations you are making against His purchased servant.

Reflect: What might Jesus, your interceding Advocate, say in your defense to the indictments you regularly make about yourself?

Act: Write out a dialogue of what the conversation might look like between the prosecuting attorney (you), the Judge (God the Father), and the defense attorney (God the Son). Use only the words of Christ and His disciples *as recorded in the Scriptures.* In other words, think about what Jesus has already said on your behalf to the self-condemning thoughts with which you regularly accuse yourself.

DAY 19

Indecisiveness

Look carefully then how you walk, not as unwise but as wise, making the best use of the time, because the days are evil. Therefore do not be foolish, but understand what the will of the Lord is. (Eph. 5:15–17 ESV)

ARE YOU INDECISIVE? Many perfectionists are. They want to make *the* perfect decision. More to the point, they are terrified of making wrong decisions, so they hesitate to pull the trigger and often miss the target that has escaped from their view. They evaluate the rightness or wrongness of their decisions based on the results: perfect results equal a good decision; imperfect or average results equal a wrong decision. They regret decisions they have made in the past based on how things turned out, rather than on whether they made those decisions based on biblical principles and directives.

Decisiveness is the ability to make sound decisions based on God's Word. If you make your decisions this way, you needn't fear that you have missed or might miss God's will for your life, or that you made or might make a mistake, or that you overlooked or will overlook some clue or message from God. This is true even if unexpected or unpleasant consequences have flowed from a decision you made.

Do you tend to overthink your decisions in order to locate the exact center of God's will for your future? This makes it very hard to finalize decisions. If we think through appropriate passages of Scripture to determine how God wants us to proceed, we often find that there are several wise options available to us. To want God to show us "the one and only, best possible, dead center of His will" decision He wants us to make is to desire more than He has revealed to us in His Word. We don't need to wait for God to do what He has equipped us to do ourselves. Rather than expecting God to do our thinking for us, we ought to use the Bible and the brains that He gave us to be decisive.

The mood of both verbs in verse 17 of our text today is imperative: "*Do not be foolish*, but *understand* what the will of the Lord is." This means God requires us to understand what He wants for us. If He requires us to know His will, we should expect Him to give us the wisdom, power, and ability to figure it out. He has given us the Holy Scriptures and the Holy Spirit to guide us in our decision-making. This should give us confidence that we can, in fact, figure out what He wants us to do in all kinds of circumstances.

May the Lord increase your confidence in His sufficient Word as you increasingly learn to seek His will in His Word.

Reflect: What decisions in life do you most hesitate to make due to fear of making the wrong decisions? In what ways have you been expecting God to give you guidance apart from His Word?

Act: Memorize our text for today and begin to meditate on its applications for your life.

DAY 20

That's Unacceptable!

The one who eats is not to regard with contempt the one who does not eat, and the one who does not eat is not to judge the one who eats, for God has accepted him. (Rom. 14:3 NASB)

MERRIAM-WEBSTER'S DICTIONARY DEFINES perfectionism as "a disposition to regard anything short of perfection as unacceptable."[1] But unacceptable to whom? Who ultimately has the right to declare anything unacceptable besides God?

"Ultimately, yes," you say. "But lots of people can make that pronouncement. Teachers, bosses, parents, professors—really all those who exercise authority over another—have the right to declare something unacceptable."

Fair enough, but what is the standard by which something should be labeled *unacceptable*? Is the standard of acceptability always perfection? Is it really true that in most situations in life anything less than perfect is unacceptable?

Some things must be exact. Take, for example, measurements of all kinds: an ounce, a tablespoon, an inch, a mile, a year, a minute. There are perfect standards for all these things. But for everyday usage, an ounce of sugar doesn't have to be an exact ounce and a mile doesn't have to be an exact mile. When was the last time you ate your favorite dessert and declared it unacceptable because it lacked 1/8 of a teaspoon of sugar? When was the last time you complained to the state department of highways because the exit ramp was a hundred feet short of the "exit 1 mile" sign?

Our passage today teaches that since God has accepted those who are in Christ, we should not judge or hold in contempt fellow Christians whose consciences are programmed differently from ours in areas that are not clearly delineated in Scripture. This means we should not say that something is "unacceptable" if God has not declared it to be so. Rather, we should show tolerance to our brothers and sisters in Christ.

Perfectionists often emphatically declare something to be unacceptable if they deem it to be substandard—not according to God's laws but to their own subjective ones.[2] When they make such declarations about others, we rightly say they are being legalistic. When they make such declarations about themselves, they are also being perfectionistic.

God has accepted us in Christ, though we are far less than perfect. We are to accept other believers, knowing that they too are far from perfect. The essence of legalism is imposing a standard on others in the form of man-made rules. Perfectionism often grows out of legalism. Strictly speaking, it is not a sin to come up with personal ideals not delineated in Scripture—for example, by seeking to exercise every day or answer emails within a certain time frame—but we must be sure that our motives and reasons for doing so are God-honoring and not self-serving.

Reflect: How regularly do you declare something to be unacceptable that God says is good, acceptable, or satisfactory? What are your reasons and motives for doing so? In what contexts are you most likely to make these kinds of judgments about yourself and others?

Act: Make a list of the top five non-sinful things you are most likely to deem unacceptable for others. Now do the same thing for yourself. Search the Scriptures to see if and when it would be acceptable in God's eyes to call such things unacceptable. If you are willing, share your two lists with your pastor or a mature Christian friend.

DAY 21

Is It Always Wrong to Strive for Perfection?

Not that I have already obtained it or have already become perfect, but I press on so that I may lay hold of that for which also I was laid hold of by Christ Jesus. (Phil. 3:12)

THE ANSWER TO today's title is "No, it is not necessarily wrong to strive for perfection." So often, people who come to see me ask, "Is it a sin to . . . ?" My response is "That depends. You tell me what your motives for doing it are, and I will tell you whether or not it is a sin."

To pursue something or, as our text puts it, to "press on" toward something, can be a very good thing. My daughter, Gabriella, is an artist. As she strives for perfection, she sometimes wonders if she has stepped over the line from pursuing excellence into idolatrous perfectionism. She thinks some people are gifted with the ability to notice things that other people don't. They see imperfections that others might not. For example, have you ever known someone with perfect pitch? They can pick up on (and are often bothered by) little things most of us aren't able to perceive. They would be troubled by things the rest of us think are flawless.

There is probably a range of "perfection" in many areas of life.[1] In the culinary world, for example, this range is somewhat subjective. I have eaten many bowls of bouillabaisse in my lifetime, most of which were amazing even though they were not identical. Probably only two or three of them I would have rated as perfect. The others were very good but didn't deserve my "perfecto" rating. When I make my own bouillabaisse, I strive to concoct the perfect pot but usually fail. I strive for perfection but am not profoundly disappointed if my bouillabaisse is less than perfect. Why? Because it is still very good.

Am I sinning when I strive to make the perfect pizza, knowing that I may not always be able to do so? Again, it depends on my motives. Do I want to glorify God for allowing me to enjoy, and have my friends enjoy, a special treat? Or am I trying to impress my friends by serving them the absolute best pizza they have ever eaten?[2] How disappointed am I going to be if the pizza turns out to be less than perfect?

In our text for today, Paul is using the analogy of a race: "I do not consider myself as having laid hold of it yet, but one thing I do: forgetting what lies behind and reaching forward to what lies ahead, I press on toward the goal for the prize of the upward call of God in Christ Jesus" (Phil. 3:13–14). He has been put in a race. He is on course. He has already run many miles. He wants to finish. His eyes are on the prize. He presses on doggedly toward the finish line. His motives are right. What are they? "That I may know Him and the power of His resurrection and the fellowship of His sufferings, being conformed to His death, in order that I may attain to the resurrection from the dead" (vv. 10–11).

What about your motives? What motivates you to strive for perfection? Is it some selfish desire, such as earning Brownie points with God or artificially bolstering your reputation? Or can you say with relative certainty that the overarching motive of your perfectionism is the glory of God and the well-being of your neighbor?

Reflect: What are the areas in your life in which you strive for perfection with proper motivation? What are the areas in which your motivation may be selfish?

Act: Take a few moments to consider the kinds of things that should motivate your desire to excel. Pray daily that the Lord will help you to pursue the right things with the right motives.

DAY 22

Fear versus Love

There is no fear in love; but perfect love casts out fear, because fear involves punishment, and the one who fears is not perfected in love. (1 John 4:18)

Perfectionists are, more often than not, self-focused and fearful individuals.

"Really, Lou? Tell me I'm selfish. What a way to start my day!"

Let me ask you a question. How often do you find yourself so distracted by your own desire to do things perfectly that you are hindered or prevented from ministering to others?

"Okay, you made your point about the self-focused part, but why do you say I might be fearful?"

Because fear and selfishness are different sides of the same coin.[1]

People who are selfish *tend* to be fearful. People who are fearful are *necessarily* selfish—or at least self-focused. Perhaps the best way to demonstrate this is by studying the antithesis of both sins. According to today's Scripture text, the remedy to sinful fear is *love.*

But love is also the antidote to the sin of selfishness. According to 1 Corinthians 13:5, love "does not seek its own [way]." It is not selfish.

Try looking at it as an equation:

Fear is the opposite of *love.*

Love is the opposite of *selfishness.*

When love is "factored out" from both sides of the equation, the relationship between fear and selfishness becomes apparent.

Fear is *selfishness.*

We can also demonstrate the same biblical relationship between fear and selfishness grammatically. Consider these definitions.

Love is being more concerned with what I can *give* than with what I can get.

Selfishness is being more concerned with what I can *get* than with what I can give.

Fear is being more concerned with what I might *lose* than with what I can give.

Love involves meeting the needs of others without being motivated by some kind of personal reward.

Reflect: What fears are driving your desires to be perfect (for example, fear of failure, rejection, conflict, embarrassment, being judged or misunderstood)? How would focusing on meeting the needs of those around you help you overcome those fears?

Act: Make a list of self-focused thoughts that keep you from seeing and meeting the needs of those around you. Write a list of questions that you can ask yourself about those around you that will help you focus your attention on meeting their needs rather than worrying over your own performance.

Act: Confess your self-focused thoughts to the Lord and ask Him to help you to put to death those thoughts (see 2 Cor. 10:5). By faith, you can begin to do so.

DAY 23

Making Mistakes Is Not Terrible

We all stumble in many ways. If anyone does not stumble in what he says, he is a perfect man, able to bridle the entire body as well. (James 3:2)

For a righteous man falls seven times, and rises again, but the wicked will stumble in calamity. (Prov. 24:16)

MANY PERFECTIONISTS LIVE in fear of making mistakes. Some people reason, "I would almost rather have my right arm torn off than make a mistake." But making mistakes is a normal part of life for the inhabitants of a fallen world, and God delights in using our mistakes to glorify Himself. Paul was able to say, "I am well content with weaknesses, with insults, with distresses, with persecutions and hardships, for the sake of Christ, for when I am weak, then I am strong" (2 Cor. 12:10).

At the root of a fear of making mistakes is usually a greater one: the fear of failure. If making mistakes is a miserable experience for all-or-nothing thinkers, the thought of being a failure—or even being seen as one—is excruciating.

Our texts today tell us that *everyone* makes mistakes. Everyone fails. Even the righteous. Even an apostle of Christ. James included himself as a fellow stumbler when he used the word *we*. "We all stumble in *many* ways." And he wasn't the only apostle to stumble. Peter denied his relationship with the Lord and was forgiven and restored, then fell into hypocrisy by withdrawing from the Gentiles when certain Jews from Jerusalem came to visit. Paul had to publicly rebuke him for this failure. Even the apostle Paul had to apologize for pronouncing a curse on the high priest before he realized who he was (see Acts 23:3–5).

Our second text says that when the righteous falls, he will rise again. Psalm 37 expands on this idea: "The footsteps of a man are established by Yahweh, and He delights in his way. When he falls, he will not be hurled headlong, because Yahweh is the One who sustains his hand" (vv. 23–24).

God uses our failures and imperfections to make us more holy and mature in Christ. To be afraid of failure is to resist opportunities to grow, for our maturing will not happen apart from stumbling. If you want to be mature, you will have to lose your fear of failure. May God give you the grace to look to Him and let go of your fear.

Reflect: How often do you thank the Lord for allowing you to fail in the perfectionistic standards you have set for yourself? In what perfectionistic area of your life are you most afraid of failing? How does that fear keep you from growing as a Christian?

Act: Take a moment right now and thank the Lord for the last two or three failures He has allowed you to experience. List the ways He has used those failures to "perfect" you.

DAY 24

Fear of Rejection

He was despised and forsaken of men, a man of sorrows and acquainted with grief; and like one from whom men hide their face He was despised, and we did not esteem Him. (Isa. 53:3)

WHILE STUDYING PERFECTIONISM from a biblical perspective, I came across an intriguing definition: "Perfectionism is the belief that if we live perfect, look perfect, and act perfect, we can minimize or avoid the pain of blame, judgment, and shame. It's a shield. It's a twenty-ton shield that we lug around thinking it will protect us when, in fact, it's the thing that's really preventing us from flight."[1]

As I analyzed this secular definition, several biblical themes stood out to me. The first was the futility of the attempt to circumvent certain inevitable and painful consequences of the fall: blame, judgment, and shame. The second was perhaps the greatest common denominator of those consequences: rejection.

Could it be that your perfectionism is motivated by a fear of rejection? Could it be that what you are trying so hard to avoid is the very thing you, as a Christian, were told from the beginning would be part of your new life in Christ? Could it be that you don't believe the Lord will give you the grace to handle rejection, so instead you preemptively do everything within your power to protect yourself? I would argue the answer is likely yes.

So, how about this for a biblical definition of this aspect of perfectionism? See if it describes you. *Perfectionism is attempting to preemptively avoid experiences of rejection by exacting unreasonable and burdensome demands on myself that are above and beyond what the Lord requires of me.*

Our passage today speaks of our Lord and Savior Jesus Christ and the fact that He was rejected, disrespected, held in contempt, and shunned. He experienced great sorrow and suffering. He was the stone that the builders *rejected* (see Ps. 118:22). And, remember, He really was *perfect*!

Should we not be prepared to experience some of His rejection? Yes! Jesus warned us, "A disciple is not above his teacher, nor a slave above his master. It is enough for the disciple that he become like his teacher, and the slave like his master. If they have called the head of the house Beelzebul, how much more the members of his household! Therefore do not fear them" (Matt. 10:24–26).

"But Lou, isn't this kind of suffering supposed to be the result of my suffering for righteousness's sake? I think I could handle rejection better if I knew I was going to be rejected for the gospel. I mean, I think I'm better prepared for that kind of rejection."

Are you? If so, that is great. If not, maybe you should consider spending more time thinking about preparing for that kind of rejection. Perhaps if you did more of this, your fear of rejection over lesser, temporal things would diminish.

Reflect: What forms of rejection do you fear the most? To what degree are your perfectionistic behaviors related to avoiding each form of rejection?

Act: Read through one of the gospels, looking for times when Christ was rejected and seeing how He responded to each form of rejection. Compare and contrast His attitude and responses to your own.

DAY 25

Why Are You a Perfectionist?

Search me, O God, and know my heart; try me and know my anxious thoughts. (Ps. 139:23)

YOUR SPIRITUAL PROBLEM has no deeper level than your heart. When you are anxious and fretful, your best step, as we see in today's passage, is to turn to God and ask for His insight. So, what are the underlying ruminations of the perfectionist? As you read through the desires below, ask the God who knows your heart to help you to identify any that are applicable to your situation.

Desire for achievement or accomplishment. As we saw on day 6, the Bible says it is good for us to enjoy the fruit of our labor (see Eccl. 5:18–19). It is good for us to want to successfully accomplish our goals. But like all lawful desires, the desire to achieve can become inordinate. That is, we can want to achieve so intensely that our desire to please and glorify God is eclipsed.

Desire for approval. A struggle with perfectionism may be rooted in an inordinate desire for the approval of others. Rather than making decisions based on what would please God, people-pleasers make decisions based on what would impress the men and women around them. They are focused on their own reputation as they prioritize their tasks and make every decision.

Desire to succeed or fear of failure. The best way to protect ourselves against failure (a fate worse than death to the perfectionist) is to prove to ourselves and others that we can do things better than most people. Again, striving after success more than faithfulness leads most well-meaning people in the wrong direction. God's definition of "success" is much different from ours (see Josh. 1:8; Luke 9:48).

Suspicion toward God. Perhaps you never considered this, but could it be that you are actually suspicious of God? Rather than believing the best about Him as 1 Corinthians 13:7 requires, worriers put the worst possible spin on why He does what He does.

Bad theology. It's not exactly a motive, but bad theology can be a source of, or an exacerbating factor in, temptation for all-or-nothing thinkers. Seeing God primarily as a judge rather than as a loving heavenly Father, for example, or exalting and following self-imposed man-made rules as if they were God-given commands, or not believing in or living in accordance with God's goodness or sovereignty, can all contribute to perfectionism.

Inordinate fear of spiritual moral declension. However, abandoning perfectionism in order to be "perfect" or mature in God's eyes does not require abolishing the desire to be good at what you do, lowering high standards necessary to excel in your vocation, training yourself to be content with mediocrity, ceasing to grow or succeed, or ceasing all attempts to improve as a person.

As you ask God to search your heart, remember that He is also the one who can rescue you from these anxious thoughts and false beliefs and give you the ability to change.

Reflect: Can you think of any other thought patterns, motives, or incorrect theologies that might be a factor in your all-or-nothing thinking?

Act: Discuss this checklist with your pastor or trusted friend and ask her or him to help you identify other factors.

DAY 26

Are You a Pushy Perfectionist?

I, the prisoner in the Lord, exhort you to walk worthy of the calling with which you have been called, with all humility and gentleness, with patience, bearing with one another in love, being diligent to keep the unity of the Spirit in the bond of peace. (Eph. 4:1–3)

ON DAY 3, I jokingly identified a perfectionist as "someone who takes great pains and gives them to others." The humor of this often-cited line is due to the fact not just that perfectionists can make life difficult for those who have to interact with them but that everyone seems to have been the victim of such an annoying person. If you think this line is funny, it's probably because you can identify.

According to one online dictionary, to be pushy is to be "obnoxiously forward or self-assertive."[1] According to another, it is "behaving in an unpleasant way by trying too hard to get something or to make someone do something."[2] Does this sound like you? What would the people who live, work, or play with you say?

"Well, I know to others I can *sometimes* seem a little pushy, but from my vantage point I'm just trying to encourage people to do things properly!"

Are the things you "encourage" others to improve on (I know you would never "pester," "annoy," "harass," or "beleaguer" them!) improper in God's eyes? Are they sinning by not doing things exactly the way you would?

"It would certainly be more efficient if they would do things the way I suggest!"

Probably, but are you really *suggesting*, or are you essentially demanding that other people do things your way even though they are doing those things in a way that is not displeasing to

God? Are you judging them to be sinning when they are not, as we spoke of on day 23?

In our passage today, we see four qualities that may all have a direct bearing on how much misery your pushiness is causing others in your life.[3] Let's consider them alongside their corresponding character flaws.

Humility versus pride. To what extent is pride causing you to believe that your way of doing things is superior?

Gentleness versus harshness. To what extent is your communication less than gentle when you are "encouraging" others to do things "properly"?

Patience versus impatience. To what extent is your pushiness simply a matter of you not wanting to wait for something to be done?

Forbearance versus intolerance. To what extent is your pushiness focused on something that is not a sin and therefore should be entirely overlooked?

Reflect: Do you desire to be less pushy? If not, ask Christ to give you faith and trust in Him.

Act: Determine which factors drive your pushiness. Then consider which of the four qualities you should most cultivate in order to help you become less pushy. With God's help, you can change. If the choice is not obvious, ask some of your family members and close Christian friends to help you decide.

Act: Memorize and meditate on Ephesians 4:1–3. Then ask the Lord to help you own these truths.

DAY 27

An Exercise in Futility

We know that the whole creation groans and suffers the pains of childbirth together until now. And not only this, but also we ourselves, having the first fruits of the Spirit, even we ourselves groan within ourselves, eagerly waiting for our adoption as sons, the redemption of our body. (Rom. 8:22–23)

THE WORLD IS fallen. All of creation, animate and inanimate, is currently groaning and suffering. You, me, everyone else, plants, animals, stars, planets—everything is broken because of sin. Each of us is totally depraved! This doesn't mean that we are all as bad as we could be, but each and every part of us exists in a state of corruption. Our bodies are deteriorating and will die. Our thoughts, motives, words, attitudes, actions, appetites, consciences, imaginations, and even sense of humor are corrupt—like a piece of rotten fruit that is well beyond ripe. They are anything but perfect.[1]

So, to think you will be successful in any attempt to achieve perfection before Christ makes all things new—and perfect—is an exercise in futility.

"But I'm not trying to be *perfectly* perfect—I just want to be as perfect as I can be."

If you are still thinking in terms of *being perfect* in the sense of never or hardly ever making mistakes rather than in terms of *making progress* as a sanctified sinner, you are missing the mark.

Imagine a pregnant woman who focuses more on minimizing her labor pains than on the joy she will experience when the pain is gone and her baby is born. Her focus is wrong. She is putting the em*pha*sis on the wrong syl*la*ble! Sure, a woman may request an epidural or have someone coach her through the process, but she doesn't focus on eliminating all the pain. She knows that sooner or later the pain will be gone. So, she focuses on the future when the pain will subside and eagerly anticipates the time when the pain will be replaced with joy.

Today's passage reminds us that one day we will be released from our imperfect bodies and their fleshly desires and provided with perfect bodies that are free from sin, sickness, suffering, and the influence of Satan. So where has your focus been? When it comes to being perfect, have you been putting the emphasis on the wrong syllable?

Reflect: Are you focusing more on eliminating your imperfections than on delighting in your perfect Savior? Whose sacrifice made you perfect in the law books of heaven? Who has promised to remove all of your imperfections someday permanently through glorification?

Act: Work your way through a New Testament passage that speaks of the Christian's future state of perfection. Commit it to memory. Here are a few options: Romans 8:30; Philippians 3:20–21; 1 Peter 1:3–5; 1 John 3:2.

Act: Ask God to help you to be patient as you await a *future* day in glory when all things will be truly perfect.

DAY 28

Impediments and Interruptions

He said to them, "Come away by yourselves to a desolate place and rest a while." (For there were many people coming and going, and they did not even have time to eat.) . . . And when Jesus went ashore, He saw a large crowd, and He felt compassion for them because they were like sheep without a shepherd; and He began to teach them many things. (Mark 6:31, 34)

PART OF THE reality of living in a cursed world is that inevitably unforeseen impediments and interruptions will cause us to change our plans on the fly. However, these interruptions are all under God's sovereign control. In fact, they are ordained by Him. How do you respond when God, through providence, alters your plans?

Today's working definition goes like this: *perfectionism is a failure to factor into my thinking the divinely orchestrated obstacles that may hinder or prevent me from fully accomplishing my goals.*

In our passage for today, we see Jesus recognize and plan to meet two legitimate needs of His disciples—rest and nourishment—yet He ends up meeting only one of them. The disciples presumably ate, but the text does not indicate that they rested—at least not for very long. On the fly, Jesus was able to adjust His plans because He recognized a need greater than His own and that of His disciples. He was able to switch gears in the middle of His course when He was presented with an unexpected turn in the road. He was able to do this because He understood the specific principles and directives that God gives us in Scripture for our guidance. As Jay Adams points out, "Jesus' compassion overcame His desire for rest (presumably He too was exhausted). . . . Notice, however, that the most important matter for Him was that they were as sheep without a shepherd."[1]

We might say that Jesus was flexible. How flexible are you when it comes to accomplishing your goals?

It is good to make plans, but we must submit our plans, no matter how godly they may be, to God's sovereign rule. God often sends interruptions, obstacles, and impediments that prevent us from accomplishing our goals according to our schedule. We must learn how to recalibrate those plans based on our understanding of God's priorities.

Reflect: When was the last time God interrupted your plans? How did you respond? Did you do so in anger with grumbling and complaining? Or did you recognize that the interruption was God's indication that He wanted you to adjust your plans to accommodate His purposes? How could you have adjusted your plans to accommodate His purposes in that instance?

Act: List the top three projects or tasks on which you are currently working. Next to each one, write down two or three things that God might do to upset the applecart. Then record several scriptural adjustments (not only to your plans but also to your thought process) that you could make should those things occur.

DAY 29

Perfect Sinners

I find then the principle that in me evil is present—in me who wants to do good. For I joyfully concur with the law of God in the inner man, but I see a different law in my members, waging war against the law of my mind and making me a captive to the law of sin which is in my members. (Rom. 7:21–23)

HAVE YOU RESIGNED yourself to the fact that in this life, you will be captive to the law of sin? Although its grip on you may diminish, you will never be totally free of sin until the Lord frees you from your earthly body.

"I just can't bring myself to concede that point. If I admit that I can't be totally free from sin in this life, then I will lose some of my motivation to personally pursue Christlikeness."

Do you hear the all-or-nothing thinking in that statement? Why should you stop doing, or wanting to do, what the Bible requires you to do? If growing in Christlikeness loses its appeal the moment you realize that perfect sanctification will be yours not in this life but in the next, you may be holding an unbiblical carrot in front of your nose. Your motivation to pursue holiness may be diluted by bad theology—the belief that you can attain perfect sanctification on this earth.

Let's correct this bad theology. You have indeed been given a new identity in Christ. You were made perfect in God's sight when you were justified by Christ's righteousness and atoning sacrifice. So, you should see yourself as clothed in His righteousness. Through the Spirit-empowered process of sanctification, you are becoming *who you are in Christ*. This is a lifelong pursuit, and as such you will be imperfect until you are glorified. It is our new identity in Christ that spurs us on to sanctification and Christlikeness.

In other words, your primary motivation to grow in Christ should be thankfulness for the forgiveness God has given you through Christ. Sure, you may have additional, subservient motivations, but something is askew if you are so focused on perfecting yourself that you focus more on your own labors than on Christ's completed labor on your behalf.

God does not require us to be sinless, although He gives us the ability, by His Spirit, to not give in to sin. Rather, He requires us to recognize our hopelessly sinful condition, accept His full pardon in Christ, and cooperate with the Holy Spirit day by day in the process of yielding our lives to the Father's will as revealed in the Bible.

Notice what follows in the next chapter of Romans. After Paul acknowledges his flesh's bondage to sin, he writes, "If Christ is in you, though the body is dead because of sin, yet the spirit is alive because of righteousness. . . . If by the Spirit you are putting to death the practices of the body, you will live" (Rom. 8:10, 13). The verb in verse 13 for "putting to death" is present and active. It indicates something that is done continuously. Paul knew that sin was going to be with him as long as he had to contend with his flesh, but he didn't let that stop him from actively pursuing godliness.

Reflect: What is your biggest fear related to letting go of the idea that you are temporarily stuck with a flesh that will constantly tempt you to sin?

Act: Discuss your answer with a trusted church leader, a mature Christian friend, or a biblical counselor.

DAY 30

Vain Regrets

I am the least of the apostles, and not worthy to be called an apostle, because I persecuted the church of God. But by the grace of God I am what I am, and His grace toward me did not prove vain; but I labored even more than all of them, yet not I, but the grace of God with me. (1 Cor. 15:9–10)

Vain regrets are painful thoughts about what happened in the past, or what might have happened in the future, that so dominate our thinking they keep us from living biblically, responsibly, and productively in the present.[1] Such regrets are vain in the sense that they are fruitless—nothing productive comes from them.

Perfectionistic people can get caught in this form of thinking. They can waste valuable time dwelling on past events in their lives that did not turn out the way they would have chosen. They continually regret actions that led to painful or disappointing outcomes, failing to acknowledge God's goodness and sovereignty in their lives. Some perfectionistic people even seek to relive the past by returning to certain places or people in an effort to correct some of their failures. Their excessive regret stems from unrealistic expectations for life in a fallen world.

Can you imagine how Paul might have been tempted to beat himself up about the way he persecuted Christ and His church? *What a blind, zealous fool I was! If only I had studied the Scriptures more carefully, I would have realized that Jesus really was the Messiah before I started throwing Christians into jail. I wish I could redo my awful mistakes.*

But Paul didn't focus on the past. He focused on the present. He said, "I am what I am," not "I was what I was" or "I am what I was," because it didn't matter what he used to be. Paul realized that the Lord was using his past to glorify Himself in a powerful way.

D. Martyn Lloyd-Jones comments, "It is what I am that matters. What am I? I am forgiven, I am reconciled to God by the Blood of His Son upon the Cross. I am a child of God. I am adopted into God's family, and I am an heir with Christ, a joint-heir with Him. I am going to glory. That is what matters."[2]

Now, if this is the case with Paul's actual regrettable actions, how much more should it be true of your regrets over things for which you are not actually culpable before God or for which He has forgiven you? He is sovereign over all. If you are continually reviewing the hurtful events and consequences of a less-than-perfect past action or decision—analyzing them, magnifying them, and condemning yourself because of them—you are torturing yourself needlessly. You must learn how to replace such unwholesome thinking about yourself and your God with thoughts that are true, honest, just, and pure.

God always builds the future on the past. Regardless of how bad that past may have been, He is able to give "beauty for ashes" (Isa. 61:3 KJV) and "restore . . . the years that the swarming locust has eaten" (Joel 2:25 ESV). Ask the Lord to help you to live by faith in Christ, not by vain regrets.

Reflect: What are the three vain regrets upon which you most frequently dwell?

Act: Make a list of at least four things you can dwell on to replace those regrets with things that better conform to Philippians 4:8.

Act: Confess the four things you dwell on to a trusted Christian friend or pastor. Ask them to hold you accountable.

DAY 31

Glorification

Set your mind on the things above, not on the things that are on earth. For you died and your life has been hidden with Christ in God. When Christ, who is our life, is manifested, then you also will be manifested with Him in glory. (Col. 3:2–4)

I HAD MY first PET scan this morning. My physicians suspect I may have cancer. I haven't been able to work for several weeks. During that time, I've had plenty of occasions to think about meeting the Lord face-to-face. I've also been questioning the extent to which my mind has been too set on things that are on the earth rather than on things above.

And that is what I would like to talk to you about today. As I have explained in another place, the New Testament frequently directs us to think about heaven.[1] How can perfectionists really obey this passage when they focus on temporal things rather than eternal ones? Rather than focusing their attention and affections on the glory, and commensurate perfection, that will be theirs when the Lord comes, they focus instead on how they can perfect, through their own self-effort, things that will not matter in eternity: their appearance, the condition of their homes, their reputations, their work in comparison with others', the fulfillment of their own self-imposed rules, their condemnation of themselves for failing to follow their own rules perfectly.

Our text says that we should set our minds on something quite different. To set our minds on something means to deliberately and continuously focus, and refocus, our attention and affections on something. What is it that we are to focus our thoughts on? Is it our self-imposed perfectionistic rules? No! "If you have died with Christ to the elementary principles of the world, why, as if you were living in the world, do you submit yourself to decrees: 'Do not handle, nor taste, nor touch'? Which deal with everything destined to perish with use, which are in accordance with the commands and teachings of men; which are matters having, to be sure, a word of wisdom in self-made religion and self-abasement and severe treatment of the body, but are of no value against fleshly indulgence" (Col. 2:20–23).

Could it be that the perfectionistic rules you are setting your mind on qualify as a sort of "self-made religion based on the teaching and commandments of men"? Are they not temporal things that will perish with use?

Christians live not for this life but for the next one. We are to focus our thoughts on what things will be like when we see the Lord face-to-face. These are the things that we are to meditate on and pursue with our imagination. As the apostle Peter put it, "Therefore, having girded your minds for action, being sober in spirit, fix your hope completely on the grace to be brought to you at the revelation of Jesus Christ" (1 Peter 1:13).

Reflect: To what extent is your frequent, perfectionistic, all-or-nothing thinking proof that you are, in fact, setting your minds on earthly things rather than on heavenly things?

Act: Make a list of the specific eternal things on which you can focus your thoughts when you realize you have been thinking too much upon temporal things (for example, Christ in all His glory; the forgiveness we have through Him; our eternal dwelling place where there will be no sin, sickness, Satan, or suffering; being in His glorious presence). As you read through the Scriptures, try to add more to your list.

CONCLUSION

The Perfection to Come

Lou Priolo is now with the Lord. Before he finished this devotional, he entered glory. He's *truly perfect* now in the way that you and I will be only after we join him in heaven.

There will come a day when the battles against your perfectionism will be ended. When the only thing that matters is that you're seated before Christ, surrounded by the thousands upon thousands of saints from throughout all of history, worshipping the Lord with songs and shouts of sheer joy. "You make known to me the path of life; in your presence there is fullness of joy; at your right hand are pleasures forevermore" (Ps. 16:11 ESV).

Let's return to Lou's five definitions of perfectionism. What will happen to your perfectionism in glory?

- *You'll no longer be striving after accomplishments more than faithfulness* (day 6). Your faith will be fully sight. You'll see the Lord in all His beauty, and all the achievements of your life will mean nothing in contrast.
- *You won't be displeased with yourself about things that aren't displeasing to God* (day 9). What pleases God, what brings Him great delight, will be foremost in your mind and heart. No longer will you spend each day in self-condemnation.
- *You won't wrestle with an inordinate desire to be, or appear to be, better than you are realistically capable of being* (day 12). Everyone will know the real you, in all your sinless excellence. There will be no pretending to be something you are not. Any fear of other people's opinions and expectations will be gone. You'll live in the freedom of who you really are and what God made you to be.

- *You'll no longer preemptively avoid experiences of rejection by exacting unreasonable and burdensome demands on yourself that are above and beyond what the Lord requires of you* (day 24). You will have no fear of rejection in glory. Why? Because rejection doesn't exist in heaven for those who have given their lives to Christ. You'll enjoy full acceptance in your relationships with other believers and the Lord. You will experience an unadulterated love and joy like you've never experienced before!
- *All the divinely orchestrated obstacles to your life will be gone* (day 28). Your will in heaven will perfectly align with God's will, so you will experience no obstacles to foil your plans. You'll want what God wants. You'll desire what God desires. You'll devote every ounce of energy to fulfilling what God asks of you.

If that's where you're headed—to glory—why not begin to live now in a manner worthy of your calling in Christ? Why not stop pretending that you can be perfect now and instead patiently await the day when it will truly come to fruition? You've spent thirty-one days beginning what *can be* a lifelong fight against the sins of perfectionism. It's not the term that matters so much as the sins that stand behind your perfectionism. Your *fear of man* makes you care more about what other people think of you than how God has actually made you (day 12). Your *desire for control* makes you inflexible, probably frustrated, and sometimes angry when God dishes out for you what you didn't plan for or anticipate (day 28). In and through Christ, you can repent of these sins and change your lifelong habits of perfectionism. Nothing is impossible with God (see Luke 1:37).

You don't have to rely on your own striving to achieve perfection. God will work in you to make you into whatever He wants you to be: "As you have always obeyed, so now, not only as in my presence but much more in my absence, work out your own salvation with fear and trembling, *for* it is God who works in you, both to will and to work for his good pleasure" (Phil. 2:12–13 ESV). The basis for all your work is "God who works in you." Anything you do depends on God's strength and His power working in you to accomplish His will, not yours.

That's why Jesus came to die—so that your sins can be atoned for. So that you can no longer live by your own standards. So that you can have hope in what God will do in you rather than living by your own plans. So that your pride can be put to death and you can live a gentle, patient, humble, and loving life—by the strength and power that Christ provides.

Set your mind on the cross. Bid goodbye to your petty concerns and unhealthy standards. Christ can help you with your perfectionism, if you're willing to put your trust in Him.

Deepak Reju

APPENDIX

Perfectionistic Thought Worksheet

Finally, brothers and sisters, whatever is true, whatever is honorable, whatever is just, whatever is pure, whatever is lovely, whatever is commendable, if there is any excellence, if there is anything worthy of praise, think about these things. (Phil. 4:8 ESV)

USE THIS WORKSHEET to reconstruct your habitual all-or-nothing thoughts into ones that better reflect the Philippians 4:8 pattern of thinking. In the first column, record *verbatim* your most frequently, naturally occurring perfectionistic thoughts. In the second column, identify, in biblical terms, what is right or wrong with each thought. In the third column, see if you can identify passages of Scripture that will help you determine how to bring your thoughts more in line with Philippians 4:8. In the final column, try to reconstruct *at least two* biblical alternatives to your original perfectionistic thought.

Original Perfectionistic Thought	Biblical Evaluation	Related Scripture	Biblically Embedded Thoughts

Original Perfectionistic Thought	Biblical Evaluation	Related Scripture	Biblically Embedded Thoughts

Notes

Introduction: Just Stop It?

1. A legalistic, self-righteous attitude, or an idolatrous desire to please people rather than God, for example.

Day 1: Union with Christ

1. Matt Fuller, *Perfect Sinners: See Yourself as God Sees You* (Charlotte, NC: The Good Book Company, 2017), 107.
2. See Jay E. Adams, *Growing by Grace: Sanctification and Counseling* (Stanley, NC: Timeless Texts, 2003), 12.

Day 4: What Perfectionism Is Not

1. In the parallel passage, Luke 6:35–42, Jesus tells His hearers to "be merciful" rather than "be perfect." In both passages, He is focused on God's love and kindness.

Day 6: Enjoying Your Labor

1. Jay E. Adams, *Life under the Son: Counsel from the Book of Ecclesiastes* (Cordova, TN: Institute for Nouthetic Studies, 2020), 57.

Day 8: Perfection or Being Faithful

1. I have written a booklet on this subject: *Faithfulness: No More Excuses*, Resources for Biblical Living (Phillipsburg, NJ: P&R Publishing, 2016).

Day 10: At Least

1. For more on this, please see Lou Priolo, *Pleasing People: How Not to Be an "Approval Junkie"* (Phillipsburg, NJ: P&R Publishing, 2007).

Day 11: Weaknesses

1. Henry Cowles, *The Longer Epistles of Paul: Viz., Romans, I Corinthians, II Corinthians* (New York, 1880), 364.

Day 12: Sober-Mindedness

1. Jay E. Adams, *Romans, Philippians, I Thessalonians, and II Thessalonians,* The Christian Counselor's Commentary (Cordova, TN: Institute for Nouthetic Studies, 2020), 99.

Day 13: All or Nothing

1. So does the verse that follows our passage: "It is good to grasp the one and not let go of the other. Whoever fears God will avoid all extremes" (Eccl. 7:18 NIV).

Day 14: Using Biblical Terminology

1. You may find it helpful to *begin* by identifying, in biblical terms, the unpleasant emotions that your unbiblical thinking may be generating. "What is it that I am feeling right now? Is it guilt, shame, anger, worry?"

Day 15: Discerning Truth from Error

1. Remember, part of the meaning for the word *true* in Philippians 4:8 is "that which conforms to reality."
2. Likewise, something that is untrue is that which "does not conform to reality."

Day 17: Let the Word of Christ Dwell in You Richly

1. Jay E. Adams, *Galatians, Ephesians, Colossians, and Philemon,* The Christian Counselor's Commentary (Cordova, TN: Institute for Nouthetic Studies, 2020), 161.

Day 20: That's Unacceptable!

1. *Merriam-Webster,* s.v. "perfectionism (*n.*)," accessed May 9, 2024, https://www.merriam-webster.com/dictionary/perfectionism.
2. For more on this topic, please see my booklet *Letting Go of Legalism,* Booklets for Biblical Living (The Woodlands, TX: Kress Christian Publications, 2021).

Day 21: Is It Always Wrong to Strive for Perfection?

1. Only God knows what the standard of perfection really is. Our ability to judge things in life has been skewed by the fall.
2. Outside Italy (where many of the ingredients are superior), that is.

Day 22: Fear versus Love

1. For more on this fear-versus-selfishness dynamic, see Lou Priolo, *Selfishness: From Loving Yourself to Loving Your Neighbor*, Resources for Biblical Living (Phillipsburg, NJ: P&R Publishing, 2010).

Day 24: Fear of Rejection

1. Brené Brown, *The Gifts of Imperfection: Let Go of Who You Think You're Supposed to Be and Embrace Who You Are*, 10th anniversary ed. (Center City, MN: Hazelden Publishing, 2020), 75.

Day 26: Are You a Pushy Perfectionist?

1. *Dictionary.com*, s.v. "pushy (*adj.*)," accessed May 9, 2024, https://www.dictionary.com/browse/pushy.
2. *Cambridge Dictionary*, s.v. "pushy(*adj.*)," accessed May 9, 2024, https://dictionary.cambridge.org/dictionary/english/pushy.
3. I have written extensively about this passage (especially verse 2) in Lou Priolo, *Resolving Conflict: How to Make, Disturb, and Keep Peace* (Phillipsburg, NJ: P&R Publishing, 2016).

Day 27: An Exercise in Futility

1. Yet Christ set His love upon us and redeemed us from all this "while we were yet sinners" (Rom. 5:8).

Day 28: Impediments and Interruptions

1. Jay E. Adams, *The Gospels of Matthew and Mark*, The Christian Counselor's Commentary (Cordova, TN: Institute for Nouthetic Studies, 2020), 262.

Day 30: Vain Regrets

1. Wayne A. Mack, *Homework Manual for Biblical Living*, vol. 1, *Personal and Interpersonal Problems* (Phillipsburg, NJ: Presbyterian and Reformed Publishing, 1979), 176.
2. D. Martyn Lloyd-Jones, *Spiritual Depression: Its Causes and Cure* (Grand Rapids: Eerdmans, 1965), 86.

Day 31: Glorification

1. See Lou Priolo, *Pleasing People: How Not to Be an "Approval Junkie"* (Phillipsburg, NJ: P&R Publishing, 2007), chapter 13.

Recommended Resources for the Fight

Adams, Jay E. *The Christian's Guide to Guidance: How to Make Biblical Decisions in Everyday Life*. Reprint, Memphis, TN: Institute for Nouthetic Studies, 2020. [This is a reliable guide on how to make wise, thoughtful, biblically minded decisions.]

Baker, Amy. *Picture Perfect: When Life Doesn't Line Up*. Greensboro, NC: New Growth Press, 2014. [This book does a great job of showing that Christ's instruction to be perfect in Matthew 5:48 should lead us to see how desperately we need him.]

Emlet, Mike. *Perfectly Dreadful: Recognizing and Overcoming Perfectionism*. Downloadable resource available from the Christian Counseling & Educational Foundation (www.ccef.org/products/perfectly-dreadful-recognizing-overcoming-perfection). [This workshop gives a helpful overview of perfectionism, along with biblical solutions.]

Friesen, Garry, with J. Robin Maxson. *Decision Making and the Will of God*. 25th anniversary edition. New York: Multnomah, 2004. [Like Jay E. Adams's book above, this volume expands helpfully on how to make biblical decisions.]

Gale, Stanley D. "The Sin of Perfectionism." *Journal of Biblical Counseling* 9, no. 1 (1987). [Gale distinguishes between aiming for perfection and exhibiting perfectionism, then offers seven strategies for tackling the latter.]

Since 1976, the Association of Certified Biblical Counselors (ACBC) has been training and certifying biblical counselors to ensure excellence in the counseling room by faithfulness to the Word of God. We offer a comprehensive biblical counseling certification program that is rigorous, but attainable by even the busiest pastor or church member. Our certification process is made up of three phases: learning, exams and application, and supervision.

ACBC has grown from a handful of individuals to thousands of certified counselors all around the world. Now in our fourth decade of pursuing excellence in biblical counseling, we have had six executive directors: Dr. Bob Smith, Dr. Howard Eyrich, Rev. Bill Goode, Rev. Randy Patten, and Dr. Heath Lambert. Dr. Dale Johnson became the sixth executive director in 2018.

Every Christian is called to speak the truth in love to one another. ACBC trains Christians in their gospel responsibility to be disciple-makers and to build up the body of Christ. This training is accomplished through conferences and events throughout the world.

For more information about ACBC and biblical counseling resources, visit www.biblicalcounseling.com.